Get Fit

Written by Gina Nuttall

Collins

Get up and get fit!

It is fun to get fit!

3

Run to get fit.

Run fast up a hill.

Jump to get fit.

Jump into soft sand.

Hop to get fit.

Hop on a mat.

9

Skip to get fit.

Skip in the sun.

Stomp to get fit.

Stomp to a band.

Get fit!

run

hop

skip

14

jump

stomp

15

Ideas for reading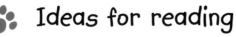

Written by Clare Dowdall BA(Ed), MA(Ed)
Lecturer and Primary Literacy Consultant

Learning objectives: hear and say sounds in the order in which they occur; read simple words by sounding out and blending the phonemes all through the word from left to right; read some high frequency words; read a range of familiar and common words and simple sentences independently; extend their vocabulary, exploring the meanings and sounds of new words; show an understanding of how information can be found in non-fiction texts

Curriculum links: Physical development: Health and bodily awareness; Movement and space

Focus phonemes: g, o, k, e, u, r, h, b, f, j, ll

Fast words: to

Word count: 57

Getting started

- Ask children what they think "being fit" means, and what they do to get fit.

- Practise the focus phonemes *j, h, b, ll*, using whiteboards. Ask children to suggest movement and sports words that contain these phonemes or graphemes e.g. jump, hop, ball.

- Read the title and blurb together. Revise blending words with adjacent consonants by adding sound buttons to the words *j-u-m-p* and *s-k-i-p*.

Reading and responding

- Ask the children to read the book from the beginning to the end, taking time to look at the pictures.

- Move around the group, listening to them blending through words independently. Support children to blend CVCC words, e.g. jump, soft, sand.

- At p12, stop the whole group reading and focus on blending the CCVCC word *s-t-o-m-p*. Sound talk the word, and add sound buttons using a whiteboard.

- Invite fast finishers to share the book with a partner, and choose their favourite way of getting fit.